I Write Because I Can

Notes On Grief, Loss & Life

Elizabeth H Adams

I Write Because I Can
Copyright © 2021 by Elizabeth H Adams

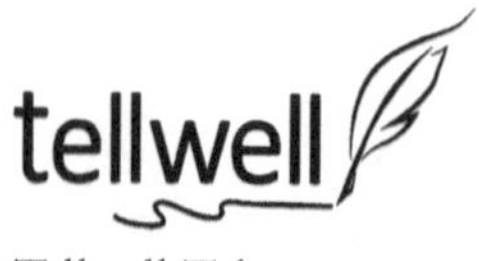

Tellwell Talent
www.tellwell.ca

ISBN
978-0-2288-7094-4 (Paperback)
978-0-2288-7095-1 (eBook)

*For my mother and father who believed in
me when I couldn't believe in myself.*

For my Pete, who teaches me about love every day.

TABLE OF CONTENTS

1

―

SPIRIT OF PLACE

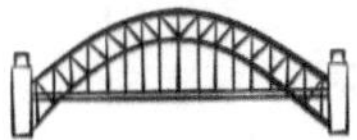

I write because I'm learning not to run against my spirit, yet the old habits want to be my ride or die, even as I'm showing them the door.

I write because today, my heart is thirsty for my soul to be seen, primarily by me, which makes me self-conscious.

I write because I know I'm a decent person, but some part of me wants to argue the point.

I write because it's so hot outside, but I'm cool, sitting in a darkened bedroom, fan and air conditioning on, keeping this burning heat at bay.

I write because I know I have it good, and I am thankful even if my gratitude sometimes feels elusive.

I write because today I crave the ocean and Vancouver, the way that there are still places I could slip away to where I would float on my back in a summer sea.

I write because the ocean and its mysteries would cradle me in its salty embrace. Far enough from the beach for sounds to be muffled, close enough to feel safe as I bob around, looking at the backdrop of the rainforest in front of me, mountains on the left, the curve of the bay to my right.

I write because it's easy at the right angle, to pretend there is no city, hustling and shimmering just beyond.

I write because those old memories although deeply anchored, are accessed easily, layered with light and moving shadows.

I write because the spirit of place, with all its joys of those halcyon days, is intact in me. Whole and alive like a living hologram.

I write because I can.

2

MOMENTS

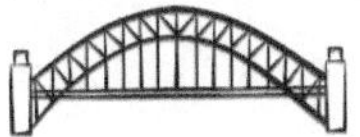

I write because I see my walk in this world as a series of tiny, unremarkable moments that stack up into a day, a night, a month, and a year, a life.

I write because it's easy to scuttle over those moments like the way we do when we surf online or on Netflix, getting lost in a swell of information, all those brief snippets of story merging into one unidentifiable buzz.

I write because I don't want to live forgetting where I've been or how I've moved through the world in a day.

I write because I want to remember that I was here. I want to feel my life.

I write because there are unexpected bursts of joy to be found along the way, kindness too.

Like the coworkers at the Starbucks drive-through this summer, posting a handwritten notice on the speaker asking people to say happy birthday to their colleague, unbeknownst to him. He was flushed, heady with the unexpected attention as he passed my iced latte to me in my car in that strange covid way, with my drink and a straw tucked into a mug so our hands wouldn't accidentally touch.

I write because today, coming out of the chilly comfort of the drugstore into the sweltering bright summer heat, I tried to get into a stranger's car and couldn't understand why the door wasn't opening when I had just unlocked it with my remote starter.

I write because it's not the first time I've tried to get into the wrong car. Once, in the olden days, when we only had keys, I got into the driver's seat, buckled up and then wondered why the key wouldn't fit into the ignition.

I write because at least I wasn't trying to get into someone else's car while roaming around with my shirt on inside out.

I write because it's something that can and does happen regularly.

Inside out all day long. In more ways than one.

I write, because I can.

3

YOUNGER PART

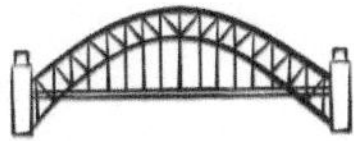

I write because these days, I feel a young part of me roaming around seeking permission to be heard, testing the waters.

I write because even though there is roaming and seeking and testing, I also see that I'm becoming a former people pleaser, and the relief is sweet.

I write because in the end, I know it's all between me and me, and this too is sweet where it once was bitter.

I write, because I can.

4

TIN TUBS & FLOWERS

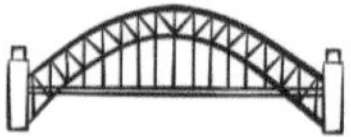

I write because, several years back, in Vancouver, a riot broke out after a Stanley Cup hockey game.

I write because crowds swarmed downtown streets, violence erupting. People smashing store windows, defiantly taking anything they could grab, setting cars on fire, taunting police.

I write because that night I was strolling in the dog park with my friend, chatting happily, when we noticed a plume of grey billowing smoke rising in a cloud above the buildings downtown.

I write because, like everyone else we stopped, and looked wondering what it could be, as people began to check their phones. And then someone shouted, "Oh my god, there's a riot"!

I write because for a moment we stood rooted in place, stunned, because it didn't seem real until the shock began reverberating through us, and we ran for home.

I write because that's not the story, though.

I write because that same night, even as chaos raged, people had already started to mobilize through social media to come together the next morning, and scrub clean the streets of the city they loved.

I write because I know it happened.

I write because I was there.

I write because my friend and I showed up at the ready with our brooms, buckets, and yellow rubber gloves.

I write because it was reclamation from destruction, one sweep at a time.

I write because it's easy for me to forget that there is good in the world and that I can make my own good.

I write because today, out in the yard, there are bright flowers in a tin tub used long ago to bathe squealing babies in warm soapy water.

I write because there is coffee to sip, nice and strong as I squint into the early morning sun.

I write because life rearranges itself all the time, loosening and tightening and loosening again.

I write because life is about beginnings and endings, on repeat.

I write, because I can.

5

DOWN TO THE BONES

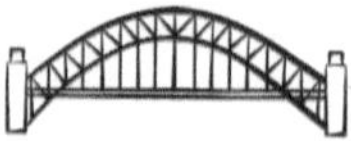

I write because we are living in an unprecedented heatwave.

I write because, in the bedroom, blinds closed to the unforgiving sun, I sit in front of the air conditioner on the carpet that needs vacuuming.

I'm so close, my cheeks are cold to my touch, the heat of the room pressing in on my back.

I write because the cool is so delicious, if I were a cat, I'd purr.

I write because tomorrow, early, before the press of the heat is too much, I'm going to clean out the fridge.

I write because I'm going to throw out the bag of squishy cilantro, the withered carrots, the rock-hard lemons and all those half-used jars of forgotten sauces with sticky lids that have been occupying space for a least a year.

I write because I'm going to take that fridge down to its bones and start again.

I write because I too, am taking myself down to my bones. Starting over word by word by word.

I write, because I can.

6

PRACTICE

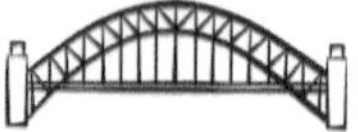

I write because I know how to hold space for my lived and my un-lived lives.

I write because it took me a long time to understand what that might mean.

I write because I know how to let loose on the page to roam around unfiltered, messy, and untamed.

I write because I am a work in progress.

I write because I am a bearer and witness to my truths as a flawed person.

I write because I am willing to be uncomfortable, to sacrifice facade and artifice for the warmth of what is true.

I write because the above takes practice.

I write because I am here to gather my brave self and show up with my words, without apology, willing to stop going it alone, ask for help, be nourished, and come in out of the cold.

I write because the above takes practice.

I write because I am here for myself now and not just you and you and you and you.

I write because the above takes practice.

I write, because I can.

7

———————

TEA

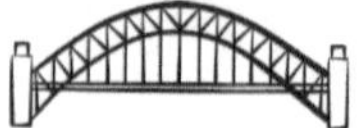

I write because there is something magical about the healing power of a piping hot cup of tea.

I write because I'm a secret tea snob, as though black and green teas were for the professionals and only amateurs thought fruit teas counted.

I write because, given a chance, I'm afraid I'd be horribly officious and bossy about your fruit tea drinking and boringly annoying.

I write because in my house, when I was growing up, you could always count on having an excellent cup of tea any time of the day, sometimes served with fresh-baked scones with butter and homemade jam.

I write because my mother liked to have her three cups in the morning, sitting down, like she had all the time in the world until she'd glance at the clock and shriek,

"Is that the time"! Leaping to her feet to get ready for work.

I write because although my mother was kind and good, if we were out in a restaurant, she turned into a tea sergeant major and didn't think twice about sending her tea back if it wasn't hot enough, and would keep doing it until they got it right. Putting the tea bag on the side of the saucer?

Off with your head! Never, never ever, ever!

I write because, for me, tea is never just tea.

I write because, for a long time, I read tea leaves, fourth generation intuitive on my dad's side of the family, the only one to make a living at teacup reading.

I write because who knew that your life was laid out like a map in your teacup.

I write because tea informed and informs my life.

I write because tea brings my mother close, especially when I drink from her teacups.

I write because I have a few good tea stories.

I write because tea has a few good stories of its own.

I write, because I can.

8

SCONES

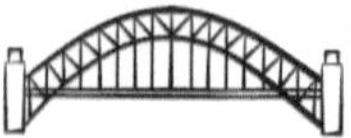

I write because I am the sort of person who, after declaring never to do this kind of thing again, takes another weight loss "quiz," convincing myself that I'm being proactive by biting the bullet, taking control of my burgeoning waistline.

I write because afterward, I immediately head to the kitchen to make fresh cherry scones for breakfast, my mother's recipe.

I write because without waiting for the kettle to boil for a nice cup of tea, I eat one, hot out of the oven with butter and apricot jam…standing up.

I write, because I can.

9

I DON'T CARE

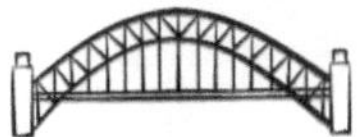

I write because I can't stop crying.

I write because there's a book with that title. As you might expect, it's all about grief & loss.

I suppose I should read it, but I don't care.

I write because I keep bumping into door frames and the fridge and apologizing like I did when I was a kid when my Monkees lunch box would accidentally graze a telephone pole.

I don't care.

I write because I'd automatically say, "Sorry". So, "Sorry fridge, wall, countertop" just a little grief clumsy.

I don't care.

I write because there is cool air on my face from the fan in the living room as I stare out the window at the pine trees shaking their limbs in a dance with the wind.

I don't care.

I write because I hear the washing machine shrugging the clothes around to get clean.

I don't care.

I write because I cry, and for a while, I won't stop crying. Until I do.

I don't care.

I write because I don't want Angels to comfort me.

I write because I don't want to keep busy.

I write because I don't want advice.

I write because I don't want a treat, like a brownie, even though I baked them.

I write because I don't care if I ever eat again.

I write because I don't care if I do work. I don't care if I don't.

I write because I don't care if you like me. I don't care if you do.

I write because I don't want sympathy, I don't want to talk, I don't want sunshine.

I write because I prefer clouds or rain.

I write because I don't care that it will get better.

I write because I don't care that I see the dead.

I write because I don't care that I've seen heaven.

I don't care.

I write because I don't care what people think I should do or should not do.

I don't care.

I write because I don't care where I live.

I don't care.

I write because I don't care that my friends are far away.

I don't care.

I write because I don't care that I used to be skinny and fit, and now I'm not.

I don't care. I don't care. I don't care.

I. Just. Want. My. Mom.

I write, because I can.

10

———

RESTLESS GRIEF

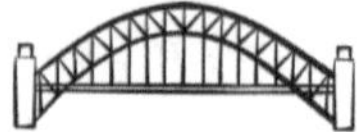

I write because today I'm cleaning out the linen closet. Lining the shelves with self-stick wallpaper with words like, "dream big, life is a journey" and "smile often."

I write because I'm sure the sheets and towels will be very pleased. Maybe they will pick up good vibes and pass it on.

I write because later, I drink the tea that's gone cold, curl up on the bed and deliberately go on YouTube to watch the video I stumbled on yesterday.

I write because I know I'll weep, and that's what I want. To weep.

I write because I'm learning about this kind of engulfing pain, how to sit with it and not drown.

I write because today, my grief is restless, uncertain deep sorrow in my bones.

18

I write because I feel physically unbalanced and emotionally adrift.

I write because grief is unfolding in a way that I have no references for, taking me by surprise.

I write because I have no control over it as it dumps me into unfamiliar territory with no maps to guide me. But, then again, what good are maps in the face of this broken heart?

I write, because I can.

11

I'M FINE

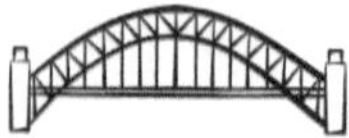

I write because when you ask me how I am. I will not smile bravely and tell you, "I'm fine, taking it one day at a time."

I write because, then again, I might. It would certainly be easier. Except when you ask, words I think I should say might suddenly fly the coop.

I write because these days, I seem to live down among the weeds.

I write because the world's noise dulls in the weed shadows, a dark green world where if I lie very still, there is rest.

I write because I can't remember how life was before or how I used to live.

I write because my world has become untethered and, just as I don't remember how I used to live. I don't know how to live now.

I write because grief is in charge, leading me deeper into the world of sorrow, and I can do nothing but follow.

I write, because I can.

12

MORNING GRIEF

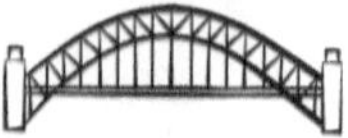

I write because this morning, I lay in bed, loss pressing me deeper under the covers. Trying to talk myself into getting up and getting dressed.

I write because I watched someone bake a vanilla and chocolate marble cake on YouTube.

How they shook the powdered icing sugar into the mixing bowl, the puffs of sugar dust, how I realized my hand was making a shaking movement along with the video host.

I write because it's not the first time I've noticed that I do this kind of thing while watching a show. Smiling when someone on the screen smiles. Shake imaginary sugar. Slam my foot on an imaginary brake.

I write because now I'm thinking about baking a marble cake with rich chocolate icing and how it might be a temporary cure against the inconvenience of this never-ending grief.

I write because I wonder how long I'll be writing about grief and grieving and how long anyone can keep reading about it, including me.

I write, because I can.

13

GRIEF & WRITING

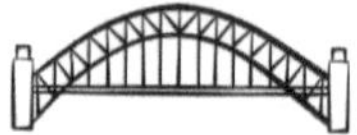

I write because tears come unexpectedly, and there is no ground firm enough to hold me for long.

I write because, on my afternoon walk, the air is clogged with smoke from the earth burning somewhere. So, I make the walk short, and hurry to get back home where I can breathe a little easier, and write.

I write because I must write.

I write because writing is how I hear my own voice to find out what I really feel and what I really know.

I write because I can.

14

PEACE

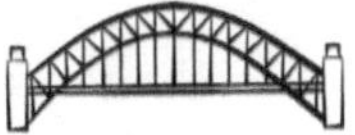

 write because today I feel compressed and heavy.

I write because I feel like I've vacuum-packed my mind and my sorrow to thaw out later.

I write because I heard this line that's rolling around like loose change in my thoughts.

"Never let anyone steal your peace."

I write because I'll have to get right on that since no one is stealing my peace.

I see quite clearly. I give my peace away for free.

I write, because I can.

15

BLUE SKY

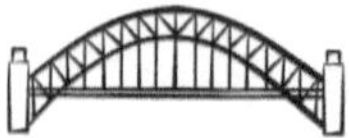

I write because today is radiant. Fall clear, sunny, blue sky for miles.

There's a mischievous wind kicking up leaves scattered around the poplar and a sense of sparky wildness in the air.

I write because today, despite the deep troubles in our world, in my bones, I feel a sense of unexpected grace.

I write because something powerful and good is rising out of this maddening confusion and disarray of the world we all live in these days.

I write because it's like the cozy smell of freshly baked bread on a cold, wet, blustery day or the sight of a lone flower pushing up through a concrete sidewalk, bright against dull grey.

I write because today is a good day. As I sip my latte and eat a blueberry danish with a knife and fork on a yellow plate, some unseen heaviness lifts from me.

I write because there is soft, luscious blueberry filling, flaky golden pastry. How the tart, sweet, and buttery all together is unctuous and slightly forbidden.

I write because I feel like I'm getting away with something and feel quite pleased with myself.

I write because today, I will take this gift of small joys, jostled in with broken-hearted sadness, and run with it.

I write because I'm going to ride these good vibes all day long.

I write, because I can.

16

INSIDE JOB

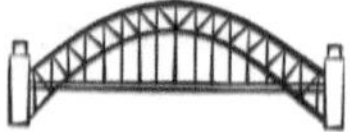

$\mathcal{I}$ write because today I have a migraine trying to take hold, the right side of my head beginning to ache.

I write because last night I chopped an apple for the salad, slicing away sections of brownish stained bruising. I wish I could do that now with this pain creeping up over my eye.

I write because I think this migraine became rooted yesterday when I took my dog for his annual checkup at the Vets.

I write because I sat uncomfortably in a pale-yellow examining room with posters of how dogs in fear look, shifting on the padded bench while we waited, the solid warmth of my dog leaning in for comfort.

I write because as we sat, I began to feel that something was terribly wrong. I felt constricted, anxious, nervy, and I couldn't put my finger on it, was I having a panic attack?

I write because today I know that it wasn't a panic attack. It was my new pal making itself known, Grief. A new version of itself.

I write because this is how it is now. How my days are shadowed by grief and its shenanigans, how I'm afraid I might breakdown in public.

I write because I might lose all control.

I write because yesterday, I might have begun to weep in that wrenching messy, noisy way, scaring people with my sorrow.

I write because I might have grabbed the Vet, shaking her, shouting in her face that my mother is dead and there is no way back.

I write because they may have had to escort me out, people whispering as I stumbled forward, keening and moaning.

I write because maybe they would have had to sedate me, taken me for evaluation, kept me overnight.

I write because, of course, there was no outward keening. No moaning, no need to escort me off the premises.

I write because that turmoil was an inside job, invisible to everyone except me.

I write because I had too many thoughts banging around in my head when I got home and too much pain in my heart.

I write because I collapsed on the bed, the crisp white duvet soothing me in its simplicity. I just wanted to disappear into sleep.

I write because I know my mother would have disapproved, although she wouldn't have said anything, she would just have that careful blank look, the look I couldn't bear, the one with disappointment behind her eyes.

I write because the very idea of that look made me scramble off the bed, move to pen and paper.

I write because woven between folds of grief, the old fears rose too, nipping at my ankles, and I wondered why I torture myself like this. I mean, who cares if I write?

I write because today, I see this sullen despair is a trick of the mind since the truth is plain to see.

I write because even if no one else cares, I care. My mother cared.

So, I did what I knew my mother would have wanted me to do, the only thing I could do as I begin to understand how this consuming grief is love, in another form.

I picked up that pen, took to paper, and I wrote.

I write, because I can.

17

INCOMING TIDE

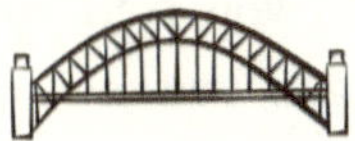

I write because I want to feel like the North Saskatchewan River looks. Steady, robust, calm flow in action.

I write because I so don't feel this way.

I'm unruly inside. I'm watchful, edgy, skittish.

I write because my shoulders hunch, they're tight, you could bounce a quarter off of them. I find myself accidentally holding my breath.

I write because my mind is bustling around, trying to distract itself from what's on the horizon.

I write because there's an incoming tide about to change my world. I feel the pull. I know I'm going to plunge into unfamiliar depths. Scattered or not. Focused or not. Grieving or not.

I write because I don't feel ready.

I write because I probably will never be ready.

I write because grief, implacable in its nature, shows me my only option is forward.

I write because there is no more time to wait for that "right" time.

I write because when you find yourself living on the precipice of no way back, you might as well jump.

I write, because I can.

18

———

APRON STRINGS

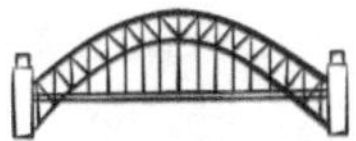

I write because I see how poets and poetry are saving me from living too far away from my deepest self, to accept that from which I despair when I peer into my darkest heart.

I write because I suspect the Angels love poets too and whisper "Courage, Courage" as they sleep.

I write because what you think about me doesn't matter in the slightest, and in the end, it's none of my business.

I write because it looks like I'm probably going to take my mother with me whenever I'm staying anywhere overnight, at least for now.

Even though I know, and probably more than most, that she is not in her portable urn, snug in its green drawstring bag.

I write because I can hear her telling me so.

33

"I'm not in there, dear" she says, but because I always thought I knew best and tossed her words away when she was alive and went my own self–important way, why would I start listening now?

I write because these days, I need to have my mother with me 24/7.

I write because I guess you could say I'm clinging to her apron strings, but as I said earlier, what you think of me is none of my business.

I write, because I can.

19

MY MOTHER'S DAUGHTER

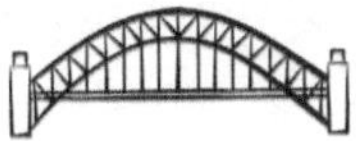

I write because my de facto alter is overtaking my dresser.

I write because I need to tidy and clean.

I write because I have zippo inclination to move everything, dust, re-organize, e-clutter.

I write because instead, I'll just take a picture, and call it art. Thus, absolving my messiness and procrastination by outing myself.

I write because my mother's mother would disapprove. In the depression, cleaning houses was what she did for a living, and she was good at her job.

I write because what you want to understand is that my grandmother grew up in a Victorian household; she was educated in what might be thought of as genteel arts deemed suitable for young ladies.

I write because, for my grandmother, genteel arts meant sewing, needlework, drawing and music.

I write because housework was done for her, not by her.

I write because my grandmother has a big story. How she came from there to here, and I wish I knew more.

I write because I can tell you that she came to visit for two weeks every summer. Her schedule, not yours.

In those two weeks, the house sparkled. Your clothes were ironed and starched to perfection, and there was a sense of domestic order.

My mother had a full-time job she loved, and I know she felt the spotless house reprimanded her housekeeping skills, and she wasn't entirely wrong.

I write because my grandmother taught me how to clean correctly, although I can't say it took.

I write because this is what I remember. Vinegar and newspapers for windows, dust first, then vacuum. Polish all furniture to a high gleam. Sweep, mop and wax all floors. Change all the bed linen. Do laundry. Iron. Scour the bathroom and kitchen. Take a break. Smoke an unfiltered "Chesterfield" cigarette, have a cup of tea. Get back to work.

I write because most things can be cleaned with elbow grease.

I write because for a perfect press, leave freshly laundered clothes slightly damp before ironing, and don't forget the starch.

I write because thinking about doing housework is exhausting.

I write because, as I said, my grandmother would disapprove; however, my mother would absolutely, most definitely approve.

I write because in the summer, on weekends, with her workweek behind her, my mother would lie on her yellow and white lounge chair, stretched out like a contented cat, dreamy with the warmth of the mid-morning sun and, eyes closed, declare,

"It's far too nice to think about doing housework," as she settled in for a lovely spot of sunbathing.

I write because I am, after all, my mother's daughter.

I write because my mother lives on inside of me. In all that I do. In all that I am.

I write because I was loved.

I write because I can.

20

I WRITE BECAUSE

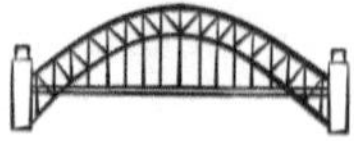

*I*t allows me to become comfortable with the uncomfortable.

It allows me to be brave on the page and then in life.

It allows me to be real in what sometimes feels like an unreal world.

It allows me to connect to what I feel or what I'm afraid to feel.

It allows me to understand what I know or what I don't know.

I write because trauma took my voice away, and I'm taking it back.

I write because someone else's child remembers how you were always there when they were little and tells you how much you mean to them.

I write because this happens right when you were feeling the old pain of not being an actual member of the mother club while getting used to being in the world as a motherless child.

I write because I hold a lot of secrets for a lot of people, secrets I mostly forget, but there are some that carry pain that cannot be and should not be forgotten.

I write because sometimes I am the only witness to that unbearable pain.

I write because life is fickle when I want it to be certain.

I write because I'm a little out there in the world, floating in the ethers, and it's good to know that I can tether my soul in words.

I write because sometimes dawn is impossibly beautiful, and night blasphemous in its dark, and I don't know how I am ever going to find my way through.

I write because the Angels tell me to write.

I write because I am scared to write.

I write because I can't not write.

I write because I know love.

I write because I am loved, and I give love.

I write because words show me my life.

I write because I am graced with a life to live.

I write, because I can.

BIO

Elizabeth Adams is a writer, an intuitive guide, coach, and a creative work in progress. Born in Vancouver, BC, Elizabeth now lives in Edmonton, Alberta with her partner Pete and their very sensitive dog, Arrow.

She loves cups of tea in real teacups, baking, especially scones. Dreamy walks pretty much near any river, lake, or ocean. Nice, hot bubble baths and long, juicy chats on the phone, but not necessarily in that order.

This is Elizabeth's first tiny book, but not her last.

ACKNOWLEDGEMENTS

Deep Gratitude To:

Mom and Dad, wherever you are on the other side, I love you, I love you, I love you.

To Pete D'amico for loving me and showing me how I could love myself.

To the D'amico family for embracing me despite my eccentricities.

To all my phenomenal, amazing friends for standing by me in good times and not so good times.

To my "sisters", you know who you are.

To my "cosmic" children, you know who you are.

To Sandra Fisher for so much, but especially for your insight, unfailing support, all the opportunities you've given me along the way and the laughs.

To Dale Adams Segal for starting me on this writing journey all those years ago and for helping me to take my writing life seriously.

To all the therapists and coaches over the years who helped me gather the fragmented pieces of myself so I could live the life I have now.

To all the people I've been privileged to help in whatever way I could.

To Laurie Wagner and everyone in our Teacher Training for giving me a way to get what's inside, out onto the page.

To the team at "Get It Done" because it worked! I got it done!

To "The Good" for everything.

Finally, thank you to all the people I haven't named who helped me along this winding road to writing my first tiny book, thank you, I am forever grateful.

Elizabeth